A World of Recipes

China

Julie McCulloch

**Heinemann
Library**
Chicago, Illinois

Customer Service 888-454-2279

Visit our website at www.heinemannlibrary.com

Designed by Tinstar Design
Illustrations by Nicholas Beresford-Davies
Originated by Dot Gradations
Printed by Wing King Tong in Hong Kong.

05 04 03 02 01
10 9 8 7 6 5 4 3 2 1

Library of Congress Cataloging-in-Publication Data
McCulloch, Julie, 1973-
　　　China / Julie McCulloch.
　　　　　　p. cm. -- (A world of recipes)
　　　Includes bibliographical references and index.
　　　ISBN 1-58810-152-5 (lib. bdg.)
　　　1. Cookery, Chinese--Juvenile literature. [1. Cookery, Chinese. 2. China--Social life and customs.] I. Title.

TX724.5.C5 M353 2001
641.5951--dc21

　　　　　　　　　　　　　　　　　　00-063275

Acknowledgments
The Publishers would like to thank the following for permission to reproduce photographs:
Robert Harding, p.5; all other photographs by Gareth Boden.
Illustration p.45, US Department of Agriculture/US Department of Health and Human Services.

Cover photographs reproduced with permission of Gareth Boden.

Some words in this book are in bold, **like this**. You can find out what they mean by looking in the glossary.

Contents

Key

* * easy
* ** medium
* *** difficult

Chinese Food

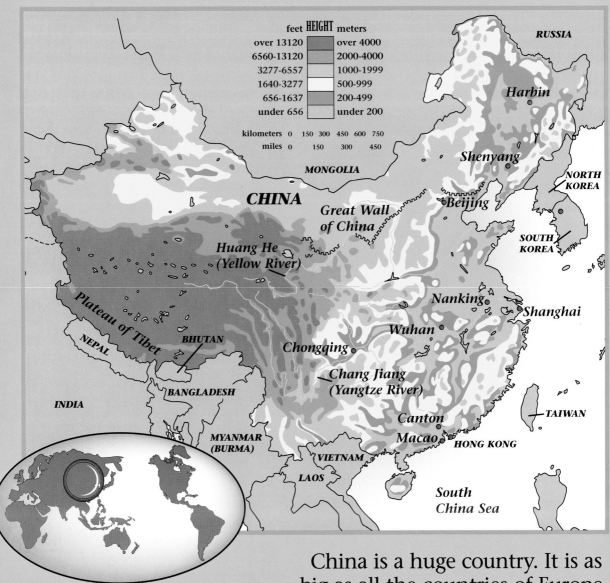

China is a huge country. It is as big as all the countries of Europe put together. About one fifth of all the people in the world live in China.

Chinese cooking is one of the oldest styles of cooking in the world. Most Chinese meals consist of rice, noodles, or bread served with several small vegetable or fish dishes. Meat is eaten in small quantities.

In the past

The first Chinese farmers lived in about 2000 B.C.E. They grew **millet**, a type of grain, along the banks of the Yellow River. As farming spread and developed, people in the south of China began to grow rice.

4

Farmers in China plant young rice plants.

In 221 B.C. E., a huge wall, the Great Wall of China, was built to keep foreigners out of China. For thousands of years, China was **isolated** from the rest of the world.

In the sixteenth century, traders from Portugal, Holland, and Britain sailed to China. Since then, China has become more open, and Chinese cooking is popular in many countries.

Around the country

China's climate varies enormously between regions. In winter, the north of the country is very cold; in summer, it is hot. The south is hot and **humid** for much of the year. Different crops grow in each area, which means each region specializes in different dishes.

The humid climate of southern China is ideal for growing rice. In the north, people grow wheat, millet, and corn. In the eastern region, people eat a lot of fish and seafood. The western area specializes in hot, spicy food.

Chinese meals

Traditionally, breakfast in China is porridge made from rice, sometimes served with vegetables or bread. Lunch might be boiled rice with stir-fried vegetables, perhaps with a little meat. Supper is usually much like breakfast or lunch. Food is usually served on large plates in the middle of the table, and people help themselves.

Chinese people eat with chopsticks. Often, food is cut up into bite-sized pieces so that it can be easily picked up. Using chopsticks is easy once you get the hang of it! See page 33 for easy-to-follow instructions.

Ingredients

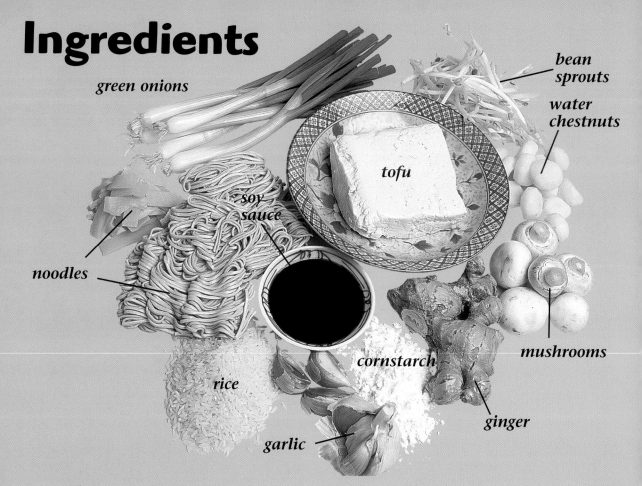

green onions

bean sprouts

water chestnuts

tofu

soy sauce

noodles

mushrooms

cornstarch

rice

ginger

garlic

Chinese cooking uses simple ingredients—fresh vegetables, fish, or meat, with a small amount of sauce to bring out their flavor.

Cornstarch

Cornstarch is used to thicken sauces. It is often used as part of a sauce called **marinade**, because it helps the sauce coat the food. Cornstarch is easy to find in grocery stores.

Garlic

Garlic is used in many Chinese dishes. You can buy garlic in the vegetable section of most grocery stores or supermarkets.

Ginger

Fresh ginger is used in many Chinese dishes, usually **peeled** and **grated** or finely **chopped**. Ginger is readily available in supermarkets. It is much better to use fresh rather than dried ginger, because its flavor is stronger.

Noodles

There are many different kinds of noodles in China. Some are made from wheat and egg, some from rice, and some from ground-up beans. The recipes in this book suggest using dried wheat and egg noodles. You can find these noodles, usually just called egg noodles, in packages in most supermarkets.

Oil

Chinese food often is cooked in sesame oil, made from sesame seeds. If you cannot find sesame oil, use vegetable oil instead.

Rice

Rice is served with many Chinese dishes. It comes in three main types—short, medium, and long grain. Chinese cooking uses long-grain rice for most dishes.

Soy sauce

Soy sauce is made from soybeans, flour, salt, and water. It is very salty, so you don't need to add any extra salt to your food if it contains soy sauce. You can find soy sauce in most supermarkets.

Tofu

Tofu is made from pulped soybeans. It is called *doufu* in Chinese. You can find tofu in most supermarkets.

Vegetables

Chinese cooking uses a lot of fresh vegetables, some of which are more familiar outside China than others. The main vegetables used in the recipes in this book are bamboo shoots, bean sprouts, mushrooms, green onions, and water chestnuts. It is easy to find fresh mushrooms, bean sprouts, and green onions, but you may need to buy canned bamboo shoots and water chestnuts.

Before You Begin

Kitchen rules

There are a few basic rules you should always follow when you cook:

- Ask an adult if you can use the kitchen.
- Some cooking processes, especially those involving hot water or oil, can be dangerous. When you see this sign, take extra care or ask an adult to help.
- Wash your hands before you begin.
- Wear an apron to protect your clothes. Tie back long hair.
- Be very careful when using sharp knives.
- Never leave pan handles sticking out—it could be dangerous if you bump into them.
- Always wear oven mitts when lifting things in and out of the oven.
- Wash fruit and vegetables before using them.

How long will it take?

Some of the recipes in this book are quick and easy, and some are more difficult and take longer. The strip across the top of the right-hand page of each recipe tells you how long it takes to cook the dish from start to finish. It also shows how difficult each dish is to cook: * (easy) ** (medium) or *** (difficult).

Quantities and measurements

You can see how many people each recipe will serve at the top of the right-hand page, too. Most of the recipes in this book make enough to feed two people. A few of the recipes make enough for four. You can multiply or divide the quantities if you want to cook for more or fewer people.

Ingredients for recipes can be measured in two ways. Imperial measurements use cups, ounces, and fluid ounces. Metric measurements use grams and milliliters.

In the recipes you will see the following abbreviations:

tbsp = tablespoon

tsp = teaspoon

ml = milliliters

g = gram

oz = ounce

lb = pound

cm = centimeters

Utensils

To cook the recipes in this book, you will need these utensils as well as kitchen essentials, such as spoons, plates, and bowls:

- cutting board
- colander
- double boiler
- food processor or blender
- frying pan
- grater
- microwave-safe bowl
- large, flat, ovenproof dish
- measuring cup
- saucepan with lid
- set of measuring spoons
- sharp knife
- **wok** (If you don't have a wok, you can use a large frying pan instead.)
- wooden spoon

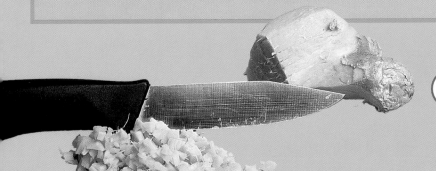

Whenever you use kitchen knives, be very careful.

Mushroom and Water Chestnut Soup

In China, soup often is served between courses. You also can eat this soup as an appetizer or for lunch.

What you need

1 onion
4 large mushrooms
1/4 cup (50 g) canned water chestnuts
1/4 cup (50 g) canned bamboo shoots
2 green onions
1 vegetable **bouillon cube**
2 tbsp soy sauce

What you do

1 **Peel** the onion and finely **chop** it.

2 **Slice** the mushrooms.

3 **Drain** the liquid from the canned water chestnuts and bamboo shoots.

4 Cut the tops and bottoms off the green onions and finely chop the rest.

(!) 5 Put 2 cups (500 ml) of water into a saucepan and bring it to a **boil**. Drop the bouillon cube into the water and stir until it **dissolves**. Reduce the heat to **simmer**.

6 Add the chopped green onion and soy sauce to the **stock**. Simmer it for 10 minutes.

7 Add the sliced mushrooms and drained water chestnuts and bamboo shoots. Simmer the soup for another 5 minutes.

8 Carefully take the soup off the heat. Stir in the chopped green onions.

MUSHROOMS

More than 300 different kinds of mushrooms are grown in China! Try experimenting with different kinds of mushrooms in this dish. Some of the Chinese mushrooms you might find in your local grocery store or supermarket include oyster mushrooms and shiitake mushrooms.

shiitake mushrooms

oyster mushrooms

11

Chinese Scrambled Eggs

People in China have raised chickens for thousands of years, and the eggs are used in many recipes. This simple dish makes an ideal snack or light meal.

What you need

3 eggs
1 green onion
1 tbsp soy sauce
1 tbsp vegetable oil

What you do

1 Crack the eggs into a small bowl. **Beat** them with a fork or whisk until the yolk and white are mixed.

2 Cut the top and bottom off the green onion and finely **chop** the rest.

3 Add the chopped green onion and the soy sauce to the beaten eggs and mix everything together well.

(!) 4 Heat the oil in a nonstick frying pan over medium heat. Pour the egg mixture into the pan.

5 Stir the mixture gently with a wooden spoon until the eggs are just **set**. This should take about 3 minutes.

6 Serve the scrambled eggs right away.

ADDED EXTRAS

Experiment by adding extra ingredients to your Chinese scrambled eggs. Add some sliced mushrooms or shrimp at step 3 of the recipe.

Shrimp with Ginger Sauce

This dish combines a lot of typical Chinese flavors—seafood, ginger, soy sauce, and vinegar. You need to allow 30 minutes for the shrimp to **marinate** in the sauce before you cook them. If possible, use large shrimp. You can use frozen shrimp, but **defrost** them completely by moving them from the freezer to the refrigerator at least 12 hours before you want to use them.

What you need

1 small piece fresh
   ginger, about 3/4 in.
   (2 cm) long
2 tbsp soy sauce
1 tbsp vegetable oil
1 tbsp vinegar
   (red or white)
1/2 lb (225 g) cooked
   peeled shrimp,
   defrosted if frozen
a few sprigs fresh
   parsley

What you do

1 **Peel** the ginger and **grate** or finely **chop** it.

2 Mix together the soy sauce, oil, vinegar, and ginger in an ovenproof dish.

3 Add the shrimp and stir them into the mixture so that they are well coated.

4 Allow the shrimp to marinate for 30 minutes.

5 While the shrimp are marinating, chop the parsley.

6 When the shrimp have marinated, turn the broiler on. Put the dish of marinated shrimp under the broiler.

7 **Broil** the shrimp for 5 minutes, stirring them from time to time.

8 Put the broiled shrimp onto plates and sprinkle the parsley over them.

Chinese Fish Cakes

Fish cakes—or fish balls, as they are sometimes called—are very popular in China. Some can be **fried**, as shown here. Others are **boiled** in water or **stock**. You can serve them with rice or noodles. If you use frozen fish fillets, make sure you **defrost** them completely by moving them from the freezer to the refrigerator at least 12 hours before you want to use them.

What you need

2 cod fillets,
  defrosted if frozen
2 green onions
1 clove garlic
1 tsp sugar
1 tsp soy sauce
2 tbsp vegetable oil
2 tbsp **cornstarch**

What you do

1 Put the cod fillets into a food processor or blender. **Blend** them on medium until they are in tiny pieces.

2 Cut the tops and bottoms off the green onions and finely **chop** the rest.

3 **Peel** the garlic clove and finely chop it.

4 Put the blended fish, chopped green onions, and garlic into a bowl. Add the sugar, soy sauce, and half the oil.

5 Using your fingers, mix everything together. Add about half the cornstarch to bind the mixture together.

6 Sprinkle the rest of the cornstarch onto a cutting board or countertop. Put the fish cake mixture onto the floured surface and divide it into four pieces.

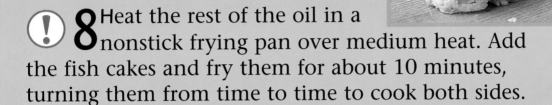

7 Gently shape each piece into a circle, coating the outside in cornstarch.

⊘ 8 Heat the rest of the oil in a nonstick frying pan over medium heat. Add the fish cakes and fry them for about 10 minutes, turning them from time to time to cook both sides.

9 Serve the fish cakes hot or cold.

PLAIN, BOILED RICE

Many Chinese dishes are served with rice. This recipe makes enough plain, boiled rice for two people.

1. Put 1 cup (140 g) of rice into a saucepan.
2. Add 2 cups (500 ml) of water.
3. Bring to a boil, then **simmer** for 20 minutes, stirring from time to time, until the rice has soaked up all the water.

Stir-Fried Fish with Mushrooms and Cucumber

You can use any fish, such as halibut, cod, or red snapper in this recipe. If you use frozen fish fillets, **defrost** them by moving them from the freezer to the refrigerator at least 12 hours before you want to use them. Serve with plain, boiled rice.

What you need

2 cod fillets, **defrosted** if frozen

2 tbsp soy sauce

2 tsp **cornstarch**

1 small cucumber

2 large mushrooms

1 clove garlic

1 small piece fresh ginger, about 3/4 in. (2 cm) long

2 tbsp vegetable oil

1/2 vegetable **bouillon cube**

What you do

1 Cut the fish fillets into pieces.

2 Mix together the soy sauce and cornstarch in a bowl. Add the fish pieces and leave them to **marinate** for about an hour.

3 While the fish is marinating, **slice** the cucumber and mushrooms.

4 **Peel** the garlic clove and finely **chop** it.

5 Peel the ginger and **grate** or finely chop it.

6 Put 2/3 cup (130 ml) of water into a saucepan and bring it to a **boil**. Drop the 1 bouillon cube into the water and stir until it **dissolves**. Put the **stock** aside.

7 When the fish has marinated, heat the oil in a **wok** or frying pan over medium heat. Carefully put the fish pieces and **marinade** into the wok.

8 Add the sliced mushrooms, cucumber pieces, and the chopped garlic and ginger to the wok. **Stir-fry** for 2 minutes.

9 Add the vegetable stock. Reduce the heat and cook for 10 minutes.

Lemon Chicken Stir-Fry

To make this dish, the chicken needs to **marinate** in the lemon juice and soy sauce so that it absorbs all their flavors. Try serving it with plain, boiled rice.

What you need

2 boneless, skinless
  chicken breasts
4 tbsp lemon juice
1 tbsp soy sauce
2 tsp cornstarch
1 clove garlic
1 tbsp vegetable oil
1/4 cup (50 g) canned
  water chestnuts
1/4 cup (50 g) canned
  bamboo shoots

What you do

1 **Slice** the chicken breasts about 1/2 in. (1 cm) thick.

2 Mix together the soy sauce, cornstarch, and 2 tbsp of the lemon juice in a bowl. Add the chicken, turning it several times so that it is well coated with the mixture.

3 Marinate the chicken for 1 hour, turning it from time to time.

4 While the chicken is marinating, **peel** the garlic and finely **chop** it.

(!) **5** When the chicken has marinated, heat the oil in a **wok** or frying pan over medium heat. Add the chopped garlic, chicken, and marinade and **stir-fry** for 7 minutes.

6 Add the water chestnuts, bamboo shoots, and the rest of the lemon juice. Stir-fry for 3 minutes more.

VEGETARIAN VERSION

Try making a **vegetarian** version of this dish by replacing the chicken with vegetables, such as mushrooms or sugar snap peas.

Honey Chicken

Honey or sugar is regularly used in Chinese dishes. Chinese cooks feel that a small amount of sweet flavor helps balance the **savory** or salty ingredients in a dish. Try serving this with plain, boiled rice

What you need

- 1 small piece fresh ginger, about 3/4 in. (2 cm) long
- 2 boneless, skinless chicken breasts
- 1 tbsp vegetable oil
- 2 tbsp soy sauce
- 2 tbsp honey
- 2 green onions

What you do

1 **Peel** the ginger and **grate** or finely **chop** it.

2 **Slice** the chicken breasts about 1/2 in. (1 cm) thick.

(!) 3 Heat the oil in a **wok** or frying pan over medium heat. Add the chicken slices.

4 **Fry** the chicken slices for about 5 minutes, turning them from time to time.

5 In a bowl, mix together the soy sauce, 1/4 cup (50 ml) of water, the honey, and the chopped ginger, then carefully pour this mixture into the wok.

6 Bring the liquid in the wok to a **boil**, put the lid on, and **simmer** for 10 minutes.

7 Cut the tops and bottoms off the green onions and finely chop the rest.

8 Stir the green onions into the chicken mixture.

CHINESE SUGAR

Chinese cooks use two main types of sugar—brown slab sugar and rock candy. Brown slab sugar is pressed into hard, flat slabs and sold in "fingers" about 6 in. (15 cm) long. Rock candy is a pale honey color and is sold in lumps that look like crystals. You might find these sugars in oriental food stores.

Noodles with Ground Pork

This dish is called *mayi hshang shu* in Chinese, which means "ants climbing a tree." This is because the ground pork looks a little like ants when it is added to the noodles.

What you need

1 cup fine egg noodles (see page 25)
1 small piece fresh ginger, about 3/4 in. (2 cm) long
1 clove garlic
1 **bouillon cube**
1 tbsp vegetable oil
1/2 lb (225 g) ground pork
2 tbsp soy sauce
2 tsp sugar
2 green onions

What you do

1 Put the noodles into a large bowl and pour enough warm water over them to cover them. Allow the noodles to soak for 15 minutes.

2 **Peel** the ginger and **grate** or finely **chop** it.

3 Peel the garlic clove and finely chop it.

4 Put 1 cup (200 ml) of water into a saucepan and bring it to a **boil**. Drop the bouillon cube into the water and stir until it **dissolves**. **Cover** the pan and put the **stock** aside.

5 Heat the oil in a **wok** or frying pan over medium heat. Add the ground pork and **stir-fry** for 5 minutes, until the meat starts to brown.

6 Add the chopped ginger and garlic, soy sauce, sugar, and vegetable stock to the wok.

7 Carefully **drain** the noodles and add them to the wok. Reduce the heat and **simmer** the mixture for about 15 minutes, until most of the liquid is gone.

8 Cut the tops and bottoms off the green onions and finely chop the rest.

9 Spoon the pork and noodle mixture onto two plates and sprinkle the chopped green onions over it.

NOODLES

Egg noodles are made in different sizes—fine, medium, and thick. They are sold in packages that indicate what size they are. Fine noodles are best for this dish, as they mix well with the ground pork. They are sometimes called thread noodles.

Vegetable Chow Mein

This is a very simple noodle and vegetable dish. The medium egg noodles described on page 25 work best.

What you need

3 large mushrooms

1/3 cup (75 g) sugar snap peas

1 cup (130 g) medium egg noodles

1/3 cup (75 g) canned bamboo shoots

2 tbsp vegetable oil

3 tbsp soy sauce

What you do

1 Thinly **slice** the mushrooms.

2 Cut the tops and bottoms off the sugar snap peas.

3 Pour 2 cups (500 ml) of water into a saucepan and bring it to a **boil**. Add the noodles and boil them for about 3 minutes, until they just begin to get soft.

4 Carefully pour the noodles into a colander and rinse them in cold water.

⚠ 5 **Drain** the water from the bamboo shoots by emptying them into a colander.

6 Heat the oil in a **wok** or frying pan. Add the sliced mushrooms, sugar snap peas, and bamboo shoots and **stir-fry** for 4 minutes.

7 Add the drained noodles and soy sauce and stir-fry for about 5 minutes, until the noodles are hot.

NOODLES TO GO...

Tasty noodle dishes are served from food vendors all over China. Called *xiao chi*, which means "small eats," they are eaten as snacks or quick meals.

Tofu Stir-Fry

Tofu tastes **bland** on its own, so it is usually cooked with other ingredients that add flavor. In this dish, the tofu is **fried** with enough chili powder to give it flavor without making the dish too hot and spicy. If you don't like chili powder, just leave it out.

What you need

1 onion
1 small piece fresh ginger, about 3/4 in. (2 cm) long
1/4 lb (100 g) tofu
1 tbsp vegetable oil
1/2 tsp chili powder (optional)
several leaves of bok choy or other greens
1 tbsp soy sauce

What you do

1 **Peel** the onion and finely **chop** it.

2 Peel the ginger and **grate** or finely chop it.

3 Cut the tofu into cubes about 3/4 in. thick.

④ Heat the oil in a **wok** or frying pan over medium heat. Add the cubed tofu, chopped ginger, and chili powder (if you are using it) and fry for about 10 minutes, until the tofu is golden brown.

5 Add the chopped onion to the wok and **stir-fry** for 3 minutes.

6 Cut the bok choy leaves in half. Add them and the soy sauce to the wok. Stir-fry for 2 minutes, until the bok choy leaves just begin to droop.

BOK CHOY

Bok choy is a type of Chinese cabbage. It is sometimes known as pak choi. It has long white stems and green leaves. You usually can find bok choy in oriental food stores and supermarkets. If you can't find bok choy, you can replace it with fresh spinach in this dish.

Carrots with Honey

Carrots are a popular vegetable in China. They are made into flower shapes to decorate dishes and even carved into ornate sculptures, such as dragons, for **banquets**!

What you need

2 large carrots
1 tbsp vegetable oil
1 tbsp honey
1 tbsp fresh **cilantro** leaves
1/4 cup (50 g) pine nuts

What you do

1 **Peel** the carrots and carefully cut them into long, thin strips with a sharp knife.

2 Put the oil, 1/2 cup (100 ml) of water, and the honey into a saucepan. Heat over high heat until it comes to a **boil**.

3 Reduce the heat to medium. Add the carrots, then **cover** the pan and cook for 10 minutes.

4 While the carrots are cooking, finely **chop** the fresh cilantro leaves.

5 Put the pine nuts into a frying pan without any oil. Turn the heat to medium and **toast** them for about 5 minutes, until they turn golden brown.

6 When the carrots just begin to soften, take the pan off the heat and stir in the chopped cilantro and pine nuts.

VEGETABLE VARIATIONS

Try cooking other vegetables in this way. Green beans or sugar snap peas work very well. They don't need to be cooked for as long as the carrots. You should boil them for about 3 or 4 minutes, rather than 10 minutes.

PINE NUTS

You should be able to find pine nuts in most grocery stores and supermarkets. You can eat them raw, but they taste better if you toast them for a few minutes first.

Celery and Shrimp Salad

Serve this salad as a main course or side dish.

What you need

2 stalks celery

2 green onions

1 small piece fresh ginger, about 3/4 in. (2 cm) long

1/2 cup (100 g) bean sprouts (fresh or canned)

2 oz (50 g) cooked peeled shrimp, **defrosted** if frozen

1 tbsp soy sauce

1 tbsp red or white vinegar

1 tbsp vegetable oil

What you do

1 Carefully **slice** the celery stalks with a sharp knife.

2 Cut the tops and bottoms off the green onions and slice the rest.

3 **Peel** the ginger and **grate** or finely **chop** it.

4 If you use fresh bean sprouts, rinse them by putting them into a colander and running cold water over them. If you use canned bean sprouts, **drain** them by emptying the can into a colander.

5 Put the celery, green onion, ginger, bean sprouts, and shrimp into a salad bowl.

6 In a separate small bowl, mix together the soy sauce, vinegar, and oil to make a **dressing** for the salad.

7 Pour the dressing over the salad and mix everything together.

HOW TO USE CHOPSTICKS

Pick up one chopstick and hold it between your thumb and first two fingers. This chopstick is the one that will move.

Put the second chopstick between your second and third fingers and behind your thumb. This chopstick stays still. Move the top chopstick up and down with your thumb and first finger so that the tips of the chopsticks meet.

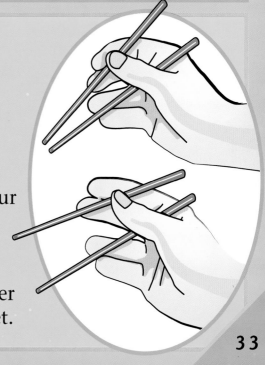

33

Ginger and
Green Onion Noodles

This noodle dish is an ideal side dish for some of the main courses in this book, such as lemon chicken stir-fry (page 20), honey chicken (page 22), and tofu stir-fry (page 28).

What you need

2 green onions
1 small piece fresh ginger, about 3/4 in. (2 cm) long
1 cup (130 g) medium egg noodles
1 tbsp vegetable oil
1 tbsp soy sauce

What you do

1 Cut the tops and bottoms off the green onions and finely **chop** the rest.

2 **Peel** the ginger and **grate** or finely chop it.

3 Bring a pan of water to a **boil**. Carefully add the noodles and boil them for about 3 minutes, until they just begin to get soft.

(!) 4 Pour the noodles into a colander and **drain** them. Put them back into the pan and reduce the heat to low.

5 Add the chopped green onions and ginger, oil, and soy sauce.

6 Stir everything together and cook for another 2 minutes.

GREEN ONIONS

Green onions, also known as scallions, are used in many Chinese dishes. They have a milder flavor than ordinary onions, and they cook very quickly. This makes them ideal for **stir-fries** and other dishes that need to be cooked quickly. The green stems of the green onions are sometimes shredded or curled into flower shapes to decorate dishes.

Three Rice Dishes

Here are three different ways to cook rice to serve with your Chinese meal—coconut rice, rice with peas, and egg fried rice. You also can serve plain, boiled rice. See the box on page 17 for how to cook it.

What you need

Coconut rice
Ready to eat: 25 minutes
1 cup (140 g) rice
2 cups (500 ml) coconut milk

Rice with peas
Ready to eat: 25 minutes
1 cup (140 g) rice
1 cup (140 g) frozen peas
1 tbsp soy sauce

Egg fried rice
Ready to eat: 30 minutes
1 cup (140 g) rice
2 eggs
2 tbsp vegetable oil

What you do

Coconut rice
1 Put the rice into a saucepan and add the coconut milk.

2 Bring to a **boil**, then **cover** the pan and **simmer** for 20 minutes, stirring from time to time.

Rice with peas
1 Put the rice and peas into a saucepan and add 2 cups (500 ml) of water.

2 Bring to a boil, then cover the pan and simmer for 20 minutes, stirring from time to time.

3 Sprinkle soy sauce over the rice before serving.

Egg fried rice

1 Cook the rice as described on page 17.

2 Crack the eggs into a small bowl. **Beat** them with a fork or whisk until the yolk and white are mixed.

(!) 3 Heat the oil in a nonstick frying pan over medium heat. Add the beaten eggs and **fry**, stirring all the time, for about 4 minutes.

4 Add the cooked rice to the frying pan and mix well with the egg.

Egg fried rice

Rice with peas

Coconut rice

Sweet Chestnut Balls

Chestnuts have been used in Chinese cooking for thousands of years. These sweet chestnut balls are eaten in China as a dessert or snack.

What you need

7 oz (200 g) canned chestnuts
3 tbsp honey
1/4 cup (40 g) powdered sugar
1 tsp cinnamon

What you do

1 If the chestnuts are in liquid in the can, **drain** them by pouring them into a colander and patting them dry with paper towel.

2 Put the chestnuts and honey into a food processor or blender. **Blend** together on the highest setting.

3 Put the powdered sugar and cinnamon into a bowl and mix them together with a spoon.

4 Use a rubber spatula to take a little of the chestnut and honey paste out of the food processor or blender. Roll it into a ball.

5 Roll the ball in the sugar and cinnamon mixture in the bowl.

6 Repeat steps 4 and 5 with the rest of the chestnut and honey paste.

7 Serve the sweet chestnut balls right away or keep them in the refrigerator until you are ready to eat them.

ROASTED CHESTNUTS

Roasted chestnuts are very popular all over China. In autumn, chestnut sellers set up stalls on the streets of many Chinese cities, where they roast chestnuts over charcoal.

Chocolate Litchis

Litchis are a **tropical** fruit. Originally, they came from southern China, but now people grow them in many tropical countries. They have a very sweet taste and a texture something like gummy candy. These chocolate-coated litchis make a sweet snack.

What you need

- 3 oz (80 g) plain chocolate
- 1 cup (200 g) canned litchis or fresh litchis (If you use fresh ones, they need to be peeled. This will add about 10 minutes to your preparation time.)

What you do

1 Before you begin cooking, find a nonmetallic, microwave-safe bowl. Spread a large sheet of waxed paper out on the counter. You may also want to wear a pair of disposable plastic gloves.

2 Break the chocolate into pieces and put them into the bowl. Microwave the chocolate on medium (50 percent) power. Every 20 seconds, stop the microwave and stir the chocolate until it is completely melted.

3 While the chocolate is melting, drain the liquid from the canned litchis into a colander. Pat them dry with a paper towel.

(!) **4** Pick up a litchi and dip one half of it into the melted chocolate. Put the litchi on a sheet of waxed paper. Use a toothpick to help pick up the litchi, if you need to.

5 Repeat step 7 with the rest of the litchis.

6 Put the chocolate-coated litchis in the refrigerator and allow to chill for about 1 hour, until the chocolate hardens.

Orange Tea

Chinese people have grown and enjoyed tea for thousands of years. This recipe suggests using oranges to make a sweet tea that is served at the end of a meal. You also can try grapefruit or canned pineapple. Have fun experimenting!

What you need

2 oranges
1 tbsp **cornstarch**
4 tbsp granulated
   sugar

What you do

1 Peel the oranges, then **chop** them into small pieces.

2 Put the cornstarch and sugar into a saucepan. Add 2 cups (500 ml) of water.

3 Put the saucepan over medium heat and bring the mixture to a **boil**, stirring all the time.

4 Add the orange pieces.

5 Reduce the heat to medium and **simmer** the tea for another 5 minutes. Pour the tea into tea cups to serve it. Be careful—it will be very hot!

DIFFERENT TEAS

Many different kinds of tea are produced in China. Different areas of the country produce different flavored teas. Some of the Chinese teas you might find in grocery stores and supermarkets include the following:

- oolong: brownish-green tea made by fermenting the leaves
- green: tea made by steaming the leaves to keep them green
- black: tea made by drying, crushing, fermenting, and then drying the leaves again

More Books

Cookbooks

Beatty, Theresa. *Food and Recipes of China*. Vero Beach, Fla.: Rourke, 1999.

Burckhardt, Ann L. *Chinese Food and Culture*. Danbury, Conn.: Children's Press, 1998.

Yu, Ling. *Cooking the Chinese Way*. Minneapolis, Minn.: Lerner Publications, 1989.

Books About China

Higgenbottom, Trevor. *China*. Chicago, Ill.: Heinemann Library, 1999.

Sui, Noi Goh, and Bee, Ling Lim. *Welcome to China*. Milwaukee, Wis.: Gareth Stevens, 1999.

Comparing Weights and Measures

3 teaspoons = 1 tablespoon	1 tablespoon = 1/2 fluid ounce	1 teaspoon = 5 milliliters
4 tablespoons = 1/4 cup	1 cup = 8 fluid ounces	1 tablespoon = 15 milliliters
5 1/3 tablespoons = 1/3 cup	1 cup = 1/2 pint	1 cup = 240 milliliters
8 tablespoons = 1/2 cup	2 cups = 1 pint	1 quart = 1 liter
10 2/3 tablespoons = 2/3 cup	4 cups = 1 quart	1 ounce = 28 grams
12 tablespoons = 3/4 cup	2 pints = 1 quart	1 pound = 454 grams
16 tablespoons = 1 cup	4 quarts = 1 gallon	

Healthy Eating

This diagram shows which foods you should eat to stay healthy. You should eat 6–11 servings a day of foods from the bottom of the pyramid. Eat 2–4 servings of fruits and 3–5 servings of vegetables a day. You should also eat 2–3 servings from the milk group and 2–3 servings from the meat group. Eat only a few of the foods from the top of the pyramid.

Chinese cooking is very healthy, because it is based on foods from the bread, fruit, and vegetable groups. Meat, poultry, fish, eggs, and nuts are used in Chinese cooking more often than foods in the milk group. Although oils often are used in Chinese cooking, sugars and sweets are more rare.

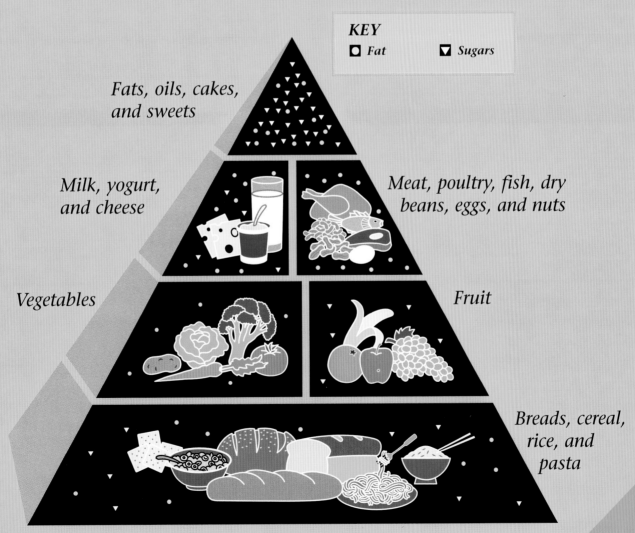

KEY
◻ Fat   ▽ Sugars

Fats, oils, cakes, and sweets

Milk, yogurt, and cheese

Meat, poultry, fish, dry beans, eggs, and nuts

Vegetables

Fruit

Breads, cereal, rice, and pasta

Glossary

banquet grand meal served on special occasions

beat to mix something together strongly, such as egg yolks and whites

bland without much flavor

blend to mix ingredients together in a blender or food processor

boil to cook a liquid on the stovetop until it bubbles and steams strongly

bouillon cube small cube of powdered vegetable or meat flavoring used to make a base for soups or sauces

broil to cook something under or over an open flame

chill to put a dish in the refrigerator for several hours before serving

chop to cut something into pieces using a knife

cornstarch powder made from corn that is used to thicken sauces and puddings

cover to put a lid on a pan or foil over a dish

defrost to allow something that is frozen to come to room temperature

dissolve to stir something, such as sugar, until it disappears into a liquid

drain to remove liquid from a can or pan of food

dressing cold sauce for a salad

fry to cook something by placing it in hot oil or fat

grate to shred something by rubbing it back and forth over a utensil that has a rough surface

humid climate that is hot and wet

isolated cut off from other people or the rest of the world

marinate to soak something, such as meat or fish, in a mixture before cooking so that it absorbs the taste of the mixture

millet kind of grass grown for food

peel to remove the skin of a fruit or vegetable

savory dish that is not sweet

set to become firm after chilling or baking

simmer to cook a liquid gently on the stovetop just under a boil

slice to cut something into thin, flat pieces

stir-fry to quickly cook foods over high heat, stirring all the time

stock broth made by slowly cooking meat or vegetables in water or by dissolving a cube of powdered meat flavoring in water

toast to heat in a pan without any oil

tropical place where the weather is hot and wet

vegetarian diet that usually does not include meat, poultry, or fish and that sometimes does not include eggs or dairy products; person who follows such a diet

wok round, deep pan used for cooking many Chinese dishes

Index